BG's ABCs

Written by **Brandon Graham**

and **Lesley Van Arsdall**

Illustrated by **Mr. Tom**

Temple University Press

Philadelphia • Rome • Tokyo

TEMPLE UNIVERSITY PRESS
Philadelphia, Pennsylvania 19122
tupress.temple.edu

Copyright © 2025 by Brandon Graham and Lesley Van Arsdall
All rights reserved
Published 2025

Library of Congress Cataloging-in-Publication Data

Names: Graham, Brandon, 1988– author. | Van Arsdall, Lesley, 1973– author.
 | Tom, Mr., 1980– illustrator.
Title: BG's ABCs : tackling football and life / written by Brandon Graham
 and Lesley Van Arsdall ; illustrated by Mr. Tom.
Description: Philadelphia : Temple University Press, 2025. | Audience: Ages
 5–8 | Audience: Grades K–1 | Summary: "This book introduces motivational
 concepts inspired by letters of the alphabet"— Provided by publisher.
Identifiers: LCCN 2024053866 (print) | LCCN 2024053867 (ebook) | ISBN
 9781439926642 (cloth) | ISBN 9781439926666 (pdf)
Subjects: LCSH: Motivation (Psychology)—Juvenile literature. |
 Inspiration—Juvenile literature. | Self-confidence—Juvenile
 literature. | LCGFT: Alphabet books.
Classification: LCC BF504.3 .G74 2025 (print) | LCC BF504.3 (ebook) | DDC
 153.1/534—dc23/eng/20241231
LC record available at https://lccn.loc.gov/2024053866
LC ebook record available at https://lccn.loc.gov/2024053867

The manufacturer's authorized representative in the EU for product safety is
Temple University Rome, Via di San Sebastianello, 16, 00187 Rome RM, Italy
(https://rome.temple.edu/).
tempress@temple.edu

∞ The paper used in this publication meets the requirements of the American National Standard
for Information Sciences—Permanence of Paper for Printed Library Materials, ANSI Z39.48-1992

Printed in the United States of America

9 8 7 6 5 4 3 2 1

I dedicate this book to
my beautiful wife, Carlyne.
Thank you for your support and love.
And to my children, Emerson and Bryson:
Always chase your dreams!
—Brandon

I dedicate this book to my sons,
Grayson and Crosby,
and my husband, Mark.
Thank you all for your love, laughter,
and support!
—Lesley

B is for Bravery

Bravery can get you through the tough times.
Everyone feels fear, even a big guy like me.

But the only way to fight that fear
is to be **strong**,
stand up for yourself,
and **be brave**.

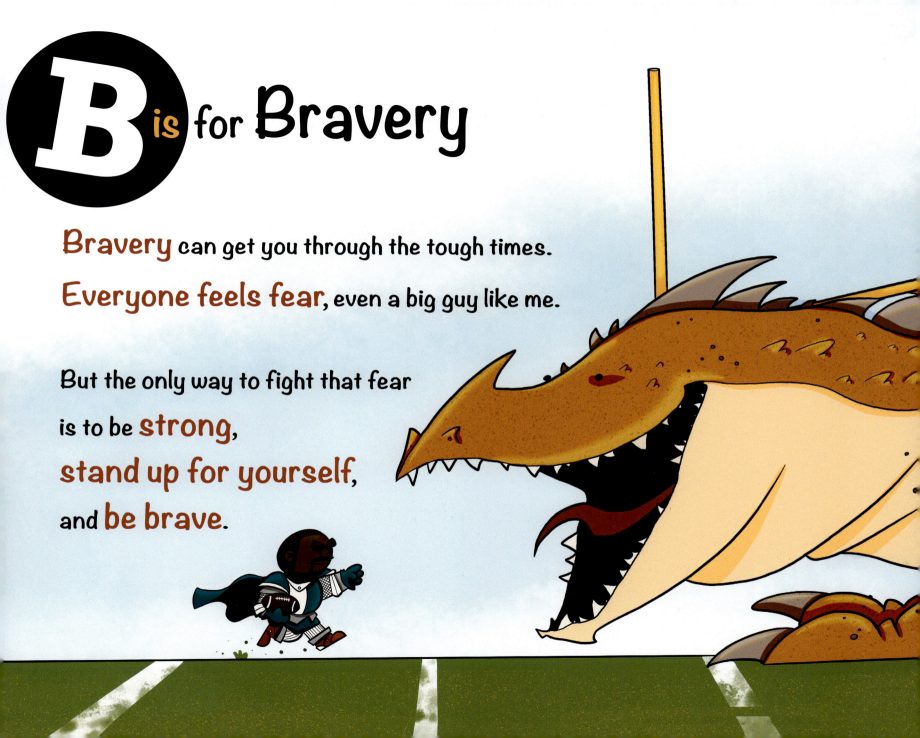

C is for Confidence

Confidence is key!

Find your inner strength and believe in yourself.

Always remember how important and special you are.
Work hard, be prepared, and you'll be ready to tackle anything!

D is for Dream

Dream big!

Nothing is out of reach.

Chase your dreams and make them a reality.

 **is for Education**

Education is so important in life.

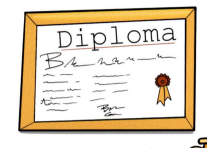
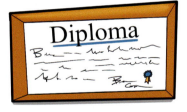

Always ask questions. Never stop learning. And remember to respect and appreciate your teachers!

F is for Family

Family comes first!

We all need someone we can count on. Nothing in life is more important than the love and support of your family.

H is for Hard work

Hard work prepares you for whatever life throws your way.

Don't run away from hard work—run towards it! Put in the work, and you will be rewarded.

J is for Joy

Joy is what makes you smile, and **I love to smile!**

Hold on tight to whatever makes you happy.

Don't let anyone take away your joy.

K is for Kindness

Kindness is caring. You never know what someone is going through. So, be kind to everyone.

Be nice. Even when other people are not, you can be the better person.

L is for Leader

Lead by example.

Show people how it's done. Being a good leader takes bravery and confidence.

Believe in yourself, and others will too!

N is for Never give up

Never give up. No matter what. From the football field to life, things will get tough. When you are feeling down, don't stay down. Pick yourself up and stay positive!

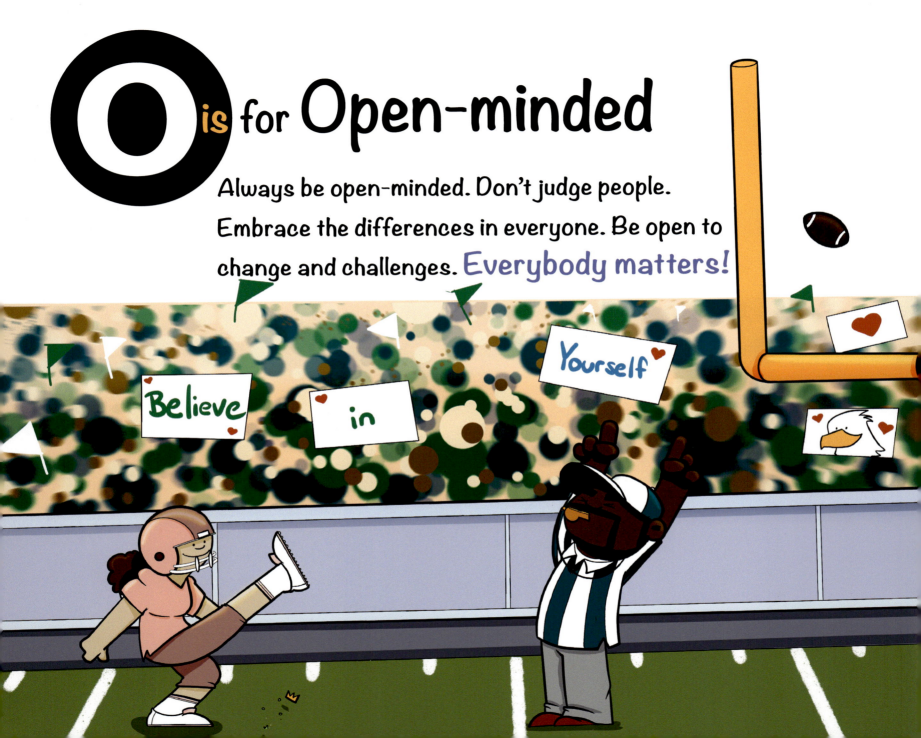

P is for Philadelphia

This city is my home.

Philadelphia has taught me toughness and the beauty of Brotherly Love.

Q is for Quiet

Quiet time is important time. Embrace the quiet and let your mind wander. Noisy can be nice, but use quiet time to reflect and recharge.

R is for Respect

Respect yourself and always respect others.

Everyone is unique in their own way. Show others respect, and they will respect you.

S is for Swagger

Swagger is built by confidence. Hold your head high and be YOU! Swagger is a feeling. Feel it and embrace it!

# T is for Team

Being part of a team means putting others before yourself.

No matter whether it's friends, family, or football—be selfless and sacrifice for the people on your team.

A strong team can overcome anything!

U is for Underdog

Underdogs can be the toughest dogs!

You may be small or shy—but stay strong and believe in yourself. Even if people count you out, you have the power to prove them wrong.

Never underestimate the underdog!

V is for Victory

Victory is not easy to achieve. It takes **courage**, **determination**, and **hard work**. Never give up. One step at a time. There is no better feeling in the world than a well-earned victory!

W is for Warrior

A warrior can handle anything. **Be fearless.** Use your mental and physical strength to become the warrior inside you!

X is for X-Factor

X-Factor is what sets you apart from others. It's what makes you different and unique. Your X-Factor is your superpower!

Y is for You

You: the reader!

You are special.

You are important.

You are beautiful.

Remember to always believe in yourself. You've got this!

Z is for Zest

Zest is your love for life. My zest is inspired by family and football. Stay positive. Smile. Find your happiness and live life to the fullest.

Brandon Graham, two-time Super Bowl champion, has played fifteen seasons in the NFL with the Philadelphia Eagles. He was selected to the Pro Bowl in 2020 and has played the most regular-season games in Eagles history. Graham's shining moment came in the 2017 Super Bowl, when his sack of Patriots quarterback Tom Brady led the Eagles to their first Super Bowl championship. Born and raised in Detroit, Michigan, he now makes his home in suburban Philadelphia with his wife and two children.

Lesley Van Arsdall is a seasoned TV news veteran who has covered Philadelphia sports and local and national news as both an anchor and a reporter. A graduate of the University of Pennsylvania, she lives outside Philadelphia with her husband and two sons. She is the coauthor of *The Mouse Who Played Football*.

Mr. Tom is an illustrator from West Chester, Pennsylvania. When not painting and creating Acutely Believable Creatures, he spends time herding his three tiny humans and hugging his "much-smarter-than-he-is" partner. He is the illustrator of *The Mouse Who Played Football*.